Drama for Students, Volume 21

Project Editor: Anne Marie Hacht

Editorial: Michelle Kazensky, Ira Mark Milne, Timothy Sisler Rights Acquisition and Management: Margaret Abendroth, Edna Hedblad, Jacqueline Key, Mari Masalin-Cooper Manufacturing: Rhonda Williams

Imaging: Lezlie Light, Mike Logusz, Kelly A. Quin Product Design: Pamela A. E. Galbreath Product Manager: Meggin Condino

© 2005 Gale, a part of the Cengage Learning Inc.

Cengage and Burst Logo are trademarks and Gale is a registered trademark used herein under license.

For more information, contact

Gale, an imprint of Cengage Learning
27500 Drake Rd.
Farmington Hills, MI 48331-3535
Or you can visit our Internet site at

http://www.gale.com

ALL RIGHTS RESERVED. No part of this work covered by the copyright hereon may be reproduced or used in any form or by any means—graphic, electronic, or mechanical, including photocopying, recording, taping, Web distribution, or information storage retrieval systems—without the written permission of the publisher.

For permission to use material from this product, submit your request via Web at http://www.gale-edit.com/permissions, or you may download our Permissions Request form and submit your request by fax or mail to: *Permissions Department*
Gale, an imprint of Cengage Learning
27500 Drake Rd.
Farmington Hills, MI 48331-3535
Permissions Hotline:
248-699-8006 or 800-877-4253, ext. 8006
Fax: 248-699-8074 or 800-762-4058

Since this page cannot legibly accommodate all copyright notices, the acknowledgments constitute an extension of the copyright notice.

While every effort has been made to ensure the reliability of the information presented in this publication, Gale, an imprint of Cengage Learning does not guarantee the accuracy of the data contained herein. Gale, an imprint of Cengage Learning accepts no payment for listing; and inclusion in the publication of any organization, agency, institution, publication, service, or individual does not imply endorsement of the editors or publisher. Errors brought to the attention of the publisher and verified to the satisfaction of the publisher will be corrected in future editions.

ISBN 0-7876-6818-4
ISSN 1094-9232

Printed in the United States of America
10 9 8 7 6 5 4 3 2 1

Romeo and Juliet

William Shakespeare 1594

Introduction

The exact year in which William Shakespeare wrote *Romeo and Juliet* is unknown, but it is definitely one of his earlier works, and one of only two tragedies written in the period from 1590 to 1595. The other tragedy, *Titus Andronicus* followed the conventions of Seneca and Marlowe, i.e., built around a single heroic figure, but *Romeo and Juliet* was innovatively different. The plot was based on a fourteenth-century Italian short story, or novella, written by Matteo Bandello, that included elements of history, tradition, romance, and fable. This story had been put into verse form in 1562 by British poet Arthur Brooke. In Shakespeare's hands, fashionable elements of Elizabethan drama were inserted, certain characters were magnified, and sensational scenes were added. In addition, Shakespeare surrounded the innocent lovers with the mature bawdiness of other characters. In truth, the play was experimental for its time, but it was well-received by contemporary audiences and remained popular through the centuries. For a long time, critics tended to downgrade *Romeo and Juliet* in comparison to Shakespeare's later tragedies. But in the twentieth century the play gained appreciation for its unique merits and became a standard of high school study and was produced in various media.

Romeo and Juliet is as much about hate as love. The play opens with a scene of conflict between the two feuding families and ends with their reconciliation. Nonetheless, the play is considered one of the greatest love stories of all time, complicated by the interplay of fate and repeated misfortune in timing. The juxtaposition of light and dark, the injection of comic moments, and the beauty of the language of love further enhance the play and make it a classic for all time.

Author Biography

William Shakespeare was born to John and Mary Arden Shakespeare in Stratford-on-Avon, in Warwickshire, England, on April 23, 1564 and died there fifty-two years later on April 23, 1616. This period was remarkable in British history in that it was both the time of the Renaissance and the Elizabethan age (1558–1603). Shakespeare received a good classical education as a child, but he did not go on to university studies. In 1582, at age eighteen, he married Anne Hathaway. A daughter, Susanna, was born to them in 1583, and twins, Hamnet and Judith, in 1585. Shakespeare went to London to become an actor and playwright in 1588, the same year that the British navy defeated the Spanish Armada. From 1592 to 1598 he devoted his talents mostly to chronicle histories (tragedies) and comedies, including *Romeo and Juliet.* In 1594, he had become associated with a successful theatrical troupe called the Lord Chamberlain's Men (later, under King James I, the King's Men), and was eventually a prime shareholder and the principal playwright. In 1599, this company built the Globe Theater. However, Shakespeare also gained popularity as a poet for works such as *Venus and Adonis* and *The Rape of Lucrece,* both written about his patron, the Earl of Southampton. A collection of Shakespeare's sonnets was not published until 1609, although his friends had been reading them for years. By 1597, Shakespeare was prosperous enough to buy a large, handsome home in the center of Stratford, and he was soon recognized as England's greatest dramatist. From 1601 to 1609, he wrote his great tragedies and romantic comedies. In 1610, he retired to Stratford-on-Avon, but he continued to write and produced four more plays until his death. In the four hundred years since, his reputation has not diminished. Although there is continued debate about whether he actually wrote all the plays and verse attributed to him, nothing has ever proven otherwise. Consequently, the appreciation of his talent and genius has grown such that he is generally considered the greatest playwright of all time.

Plot Summary

Prologue to Act 1

The prologue tells the audience that this story will be about two prominent families of Verona, Italy, whose ancient feud is erupting anew and that a "pair of star-cross'd lovers" from these families will end the violence by ending their own lives.

Act 1

In scene 1, Capulet servants, Sampson and Gregory, and Montague servants, Abraham and Balthasar, start a street fight that is joined by Benvolio, a Montague relative, and Tybalt a Capulet relative. Escalus, the Prince of Verona, learns about the fight and angrily decrees a death penalty for anyone caught in further feuding. Benvolio finds Romeo and learns that Romeo is forlorn because the girl he loves, Rosaline, will not return his affection because she has chosen to remain chaste. Benvolio advises Romeo to move on with his life and look at other girls. Romeo, however, is quite sure that he cannot forget Rosaline.

Scene 2 opens with Lord Capulet being approached by Count Paris, a relative of Prince Escalus, about marrying Capulet's daughter, Juliet. Capulet thinks Juliet is too young to marry but agrees to let the two meet at a party he is hosting that night. By accident, Romeo and Benvolio find out about the party, and Benvolio encourages Romeo to crash the party with him.

It is in scene 3 that the audience meets the garrulous nurse and learns that Juliet is only 14 years old. Lady Capulet discusses the idea of marriage to Paris with Juliet, who has not yet given marriage any thought, but she obediently agrees to consider the match.

Scene 4 finds Mercutio, another relative of the prince, joining Romeo and Benvolio and other friends on their way to the party. Mercutio teases the lovesick Romeo by scoffing at love. As they reach the party, Romeo expresses a feeling of impending doom.

Scene 5 takes place at the Capulet's party where a disguised Romeo spies Juliet and falls instantly in love. Lady Capulet's nephew Tybalt discovers Romeo's presence but is prevented from attacking Romeo by Lord Capulet who does not want such a disturbance at his party. In a brief encounter with Romeo, Juliet too falls in love. Later, they each learn separately from the nurse the family identity of the other.

Prologue to Act 2

The chorus dramatizes the complications faced by both Romeo and Juliet in their love for one another but predicts that passion will lend them the power needed to be together.

Act 2

In a very short scene 1, Benvolio and Mercutio try to find Romeo, who has climbed a wall to hide in the Capulet orchard. His friends give up when Romeo will not respond to their calls.

Scene 2 is the famous balcony scene in which, ignoring the danger, Romeo hopes for a glimpse of Juliet outside her window. Romeo overhears Juliet talk about her love for him. He then approaches her, and, after declaring their love, the two decide to marry. Juliet promises to send Romeo a messenger in the morning to make plans for their wedding.

In scene 3, Romeo goes to see Friar Laurence to arrange the wedding. Friar Laurence agrees to marry the two in hopes that their union will end the feud.

In scene 4, Romeo meets his friends Mercutio and Benvolio, who are discussing a challenge sent by Tybalt to Romeo. Juliet's messenger, the nurse, arrives and speaks privately to Romeo. The wedding is set for later that day.

In scene 5, the nurse returns to Juliet and, after much teasing to exasperate the eager Juliet, she reveals her news. Juliet uses the excuse of going to confession to get to Friar Laurence's cell.

A tiny scene 6 accomplishes the wedding of Romeo and Juliet.

Act 3

In scene 1, later that day, Benvolio and Mercutio encounter Tybalt and are already sparring with words when Romeo arrives. Tybalt attempts to provoke Romeo into a fight, but Romeo will not fight because, although unknown to the others, he and Tybalt are now relatives by marriage. Instead, Mercutio challenges Tybalt and is killed by a deceitful stab from Tybalt when Romeo tries to separate them. Tybalt flees and Mercutio dies. Romeo is so enraged that he tracks down Tybalt and kills him. Benvolio urges Romeo to flee. Just then, Escalus arrives and banishes Romeo from Verona.

In scene 2, the nurse tells Juliet that Romeo has killed Tybalt. Despite her intense grief over Tybalt, Juliet's love for Romeo wins out, and she asks the nurse to find Romeo.

Scene 3 finds Romeo in Friar Laurence's cell. Romeo learns of the banishment order and almost commits suicide when he realizes he may not be able to see Juliet again. However, the nurse's arrival and the friar's confidence that the crisis will blow over if Romeo will just hide out in Mantua for a while encourages Romeo to go see Juliet.

A brief scene 4 finds Capulet deciding that marrying Paris will soothe what Capulet assumes is Juliet's grief over Tybalt's death. Capulet sets the wedding for three days away and instructs his wife to tell Juliet.

Scene 5 takes place at dawn after Romeo and Juliet have spent the night together. Just after their heart-wrenching farewell, Juliet's mother arrives and tells Juliet that she is to marry Paris. Juliet refuses, and a terrible fight with her parents ensues. The nurse counsels Juliet to forget Romeo and marry Paris. Feeling betrayed by all, Juliet makes another excuse to see Friar Laurence.

Act 4

Scene 1 is back at Friar Laurence's, where he tells Juliet to take a potion that will cause her to appear dead until Romeo can come to rescue her and take her away with him to Mantua.

In scene 2, Juliet claims that she has repented of her disobedience and agrees to marry Paris. Lord Capulet is so pleased, he moves up the wedding to the next morning.

Scene 3 finds Juliet asking the nurse to leave her alone that night. She then worries about trusting the friar, but she takes the potion anyway.

Scene 4 shows the whole Capulet household working through the night to prepare for the wedding.

In scene 5, the nurse finds Juliet apparently dead. The wedding preparations are changed to those of a funeral.

Act 5

Scene 1 takes place in Mantua as Romeo's servant Balthasar arrives, bringing the news of Juliet's death. Romeo decides to risk his own life by returning immediately to Verona. He buys poison from an apothecary with the intent of dying beside Juliet.

In scene 2, Friar Laurence learns that his letter to Romeo explaining Juliet's deception was not received. His messenger, Friar John, was confined by quarantine. Friar Laurence sends another letter to Mantua and heads off to the Capulet burial chamber to be there when Juliet awakens.

In the final scene, Paris goes to Juliet's tomb to mourn her but finds Romeo there and assumes that, as a Montague, Romeo is desecrating Juliet's grave. A fight ensues and Paris is killed. Romeo places him beside Juliet, then takes the poison, kisses Juliet, and dies. Friar Laurence finally arrives, but Juliet awakens and sees Romeo. Upon hearing noises, Friar Laurence runs away, but Juliet will not leave. Juliet kisses Romeo, stabs herself, and dies. The arriving guards find the bodies, send for the prince, and discover the friar in hiding. The prince, the Capulets and the Montagues all arrive, and Balthasar, Paris's page, and Friar Laurence explain everything. Escalus confronts the two families with the results of their feud and the two lords reconcile with promises to build gold statues to each other's lost child. The play concludes with the prince's declaration:

> For never was there a story of more woe
>
> Than this of Juliet and her Romeo.

Characters

Abraham

A Montague servant, Abraham and Balthasar are the opponents to Sampson and Gregory in the opening fight scene.

The Apothecary

The apothecary's appearance is brief but critical. It is his poverty that forces him to violate the law and his own morals in selling Romeo the poison that he will use in suicide.

Balthasar

Romeo's servant Balthasar brings the mistaken news to Romeo that Juliet is dead. He also witnesses the fight between Paris and Romeo and then Romeo's suicide. It is then Balthasar who verifies Friar Laurence's explanation to the prince.

Juliet Capulet

The daughter of Lord and Lady Capulet, Juliet is in love with Romeo. Just entering her teenage years, she is an innocent girl with a practical nature and remarkable strength who is willing to go to great lengths, even defying her parents and faking her own death, to be with Romeo. Although Juliet is willing to consider Paris's proposal, once she meets Romeo at the Capulet party, her heart is set only for him. Nonetheless, she is wary enough to suspect his intentions since he is a Montague, a family enemy. She thus requires that he marry her to prove his sincerity. Her love for Romeo is strong enough to forgive him for killing her cousin Tybalt and to chance the friar's risky plan to avoid marrying Paris. Juliet also shows a new maturity in being able to recognize the nurse's betrayal and to break their strong bond as well as that with her parents. Although suicide is always a negative choice, for Juliet it is a final demonstration of the strength and commitment of her love for Romeo.

Lady Capulet

As Juliet's mother, Lady Capulet tries to keep peace in the family by attempting to convince Juliet to marry her father's choice of a husband for her. We learn that she married and gave birth at Juliet's age. However, she is not close to Juliet and relies on the nurse to be a surrogate mother.

Lord Capulet

Lord Capulet is a paradoxical character who can be the perfect genial host in public but a tyrannical father when he thinks his authority is questioned. He loves his daughter very much but makes the classic parental mistake of trying to force her to do something because he thinks it is best for her. His decision to move up the wedding of Juliet and Paris is the catalyst for the complications that result in his daughter's death.

The Chorus

The chorus is actually a single character functioning as the narrator who reveals the plot to the audience.

Prince Escalus

As ruler of Verona, Prince Escalus is intent on stopping the feud between the Montagues and the Capulets and bringing peace to the streets of his city. He issues a warning that the offense of fighting between members of the two houses will be punished by death, but when Romeo kills Tybalt the prince orders only banishment. When the feud results in the deaths of Romeo and Juliet, the prince tells their families that they are to blame, but he also blames himself for being unable to stop the feuding in time.

Gregory

A servant of the house of Capulet, Gregory and fellow Capulet servant Sampson show that the Montague-Capulet feud extends to the servants when they pick a fight with the opposing family in the opening scene of the play.

Media Adaptations

- An audiocassette of *Romeo and Juliet* was made by Caedmon Audio in 1996 and features Claire Bloom and Albert Finney.

- A film version of *Romeo and Juliet* (1936) was released in black and white, starring Norma Shearer and Leslie Howard and directed by George Cukor. It is available on VHS from Warner Studios.

- A color film version of *Romeo and Juliet* (1956) starring Lawrence Harvey was made available on video in 1997 by Hallmark Entertainment. It was also released on video by MGM/UA in 2000.

- Kultur Video released a 1966 filming of Prokofiev's ballet version as performed by Rudolf Nureyev, Margot Fonteyn, and the Royal Ballet. It is available on both VHS and DVD.

- The 1968 blockbuster version directed by Franco Zeffirelli and starring Olivia Hussey and Leonard Whiting is available on video from Paramount Studios.
- A BBC and Time-Life Film production of *Romeo and Juliet* was part of a BBC series on The Shakespeare Plays in 1978. Digitally remastered for DVD in 2001, it is distributed by Ambrose Video Publishing.
- A 1996 film version, using Shakespeare's language in a modern update and starring Leonardo DiCaprio and Claire Danes, is available on video from Fox Home Entertainment.

Friar John

A minor character, Friar John is the messenger who gets quarantined and thus fails to get the message to Romeo from Friar Laurence that Juliet is only asleep and not dead.

Friar Laurence

A well-meaning priest and expert in herbal medicines, Friar Laurence is Romeo and Juliet's confidant. His role is to be the advocate of moderation and the problem-solver. He marries Romeo and Juliet in hopes of ending the feud between their families through their love. However, it is his plan to help Juliet escape to be with Romeo in exile that backfires and leads to the deaths of the young pair. He confesses his guilt to the prince at the end of the play and is forgiven for his participation in the tragedy.

Mercutio

Another kinsman of Prince Escalus, Mercutio is Romeo's intensely witty, satirical, and imaginative friend. It is Mercutio who gives the famous speech about Queen Mab and who teases Romeo relentlessly. He is a scene-stealing character whose puns, such as "ask for me tomorrow, and you shall find me a grave man" in reference to his own death, are memorable. He is mortally wounded in a swordfight with Tybalt but does not die until he has called for a plague on the houses of Montague and Capulet. For those who see the action of this play as determined by fate, this curse is the determining factor. It is in revenge for Mercutio's death that Romeo kills Tybalt and is thus forced to leave Verona and Juliet.

Benvolio Montague

Benvolio is Romeo's cousin and good friend. His calm, thoughtful demeanor is a foil to the character of Romeo's other good friend, Mercutio. Benvolio's role, though relatively small, has some key moments. It is Benvolio who discovers the reason for Romeo's melancholy and then encourages him to go to the Capulet party where Romeo meets Juliet. It is Benvolio who tells Romeo that Mercutio is dead and then urges Romeo to run away after Romeo has killed Tybalt.

Lady Montague

Lady Montague appears only at the beginning of the play to express worry about Romeo's melancholy and later is reported to have died of grief when her son is banished from Verona.

Lord Montague

Romeo's father, Lord Montague, makes only slight appearances in the play, but it is evident that he has loving concern for his only son. At the end, he and Lord Capulet end their feud and pledge to build gold statues to each other's dead child.

Romeo Montague

Romeo's relationship with Juliet, the daughter of a rival family, is the center of the drama. The teenage son of Lord and Lady Montague, Romeo seems an overly sensitive lovesick boy at first. His behavior vacillates between extremes of joy and despair, love and hatred. The speed with which he forgets his infatuation with Rosaline and falls in love with Juliet may seem fickle, but it may also indicate a maturing from a silly crush to a commitment in true love. Romeo's soliloquy beneath Juliet's balcony is one of the most often quoted lines from a play:

> But, soft! What light through yonder window breaks?
>
> It is the east, and Juliet is the sun.

The depth and fluctuation of his feelings is evident in his resolve not to fight with Juliet's cousin Tybalt, out of love for her, and his rage that leads him to kill Tybalt, out of loyalty and affection for his friend Mercutio. Romeo marries Juliet to prove the sincerity of his love, but he must leave her when he is banished for killing Tybalt. He almost takes his life in despair over being separated from Juliet but is convinced by his good friend, Friar Laurence, to let time heal their problem. However, time is an enemy to the couple throughout the play, and when Romeo thinks Juliet is dead, he once again determines to take his own life. In trying to reach Juliet's tomb to commit this act, he encounters and is forced to kill Paris. In his rush of passion, Romeo dies before he can be told that Juliet is still alive. His death then causes Juliet to commit suicide also. Although their deaths are tragic, they have the effect of ending the feud between their families.

Nurse

The nurse is a comic and vulgar figure in the play whose lewd remarks and long-winded speeches provide a break in the tension of the tragedy. More of a mother to Juliet than Juliet's mother, the nurse has reared Juliet and loves her to the point of being willing to do anything to make Juliet happy. Consequently, she is willing to be the go-between for Romeo and Juliet and to help them get married and have a wedding night. However, her more physical than emotional interest in love leaves her unable to understand Juliet's willingness to endanger herself for Romeo. To the nurse, it is better for Juliet to drop a relationship that is difficult to maintain and marry into a soft life with Paris. This advice seems a betrayal to Juliet and forces her to seek out a desperate plan to escape rather than confide in her closest advocate. Like everyone else at the end of the play, the nurse must face failure and grief.

Count Paris

A kinsman of Prince Escalus, Paris is Juliet's suitor. Lord Capulet approves of and promotes the match. Paris is a true gentleman who loves Juliet and has no idea that he is in the middle of two lovers. On a visit to Juliet's tomb, he mistakes Romeo for someone who is trying to desecrate her grave. In the ensuing fight, Paris is killed by Romeo who grants Paris's last wish to be buried next to Juliet.

Peter

Peter is the nurse's servant who carries messages and run errands.

Rosaline

Although Rosaline does not actually appear in the play, she is the reason for Romeo's initial lovesickness. Further, it is only because he hopes to see Rosaline that Romeo agrees to go to the Capulet party where the pivotal moment occurs when he meets Juliet.

Sampson

A Capulet servant, it is Sampson and his fellow servant Gregory who open the play by picking a fight with some servants of the Montague family.

Tybalt

A nephew of Lady Capulet, Tybalt is Juliet's hot-tempered cousin who is the most hateful towards the Montagues. When he spies Romeo at the Capulet party, only Lord Capulet's stern restraint prevents Tybalt from attacking Romeo. Later, still feeling insulted but unable to goad Romeo into fighting, Tybalt provokes Mercutio and kills him. Then, in rage of revenge, Romeo forgets that Tybalt has become a relative by marriage and kills him. It is Juliet's grief apparently over Tybalt's death that gives her father the excuse to bring joy to the house with a wedding for Juliet and Paris. This turn of events precipitates the tragic plan of faked death that leads to the suicides of both Romeo and Juliet.

Themes

The Power and Passion of Love and Hate

Although *Romeo and Juliet* is considered one of the world's greatest love stories, it can be argued that the love story is only a vehicle for the resolution of the story about hate, that is, the feud between the two families. After all, the story starts with a street fight between Montague and Capulet servants and ends with a peace agreement between the two lords. The power of hate is illustrated in the first scene by the exhibition of enmity between servants of the two families. The extent of the hatred has grown from the family itself to its servants. The power of love is seen, of course, in the determination of Romeo and Juliet to defy their families and be together. They love their parents, but the hate between the families causes the young couple to hate those who would keep them apart. The passion of Tybalt's hate is seen in his inability to forget about the party crashing. Even though his uncle talks him out of a fight that night, the next morning he sends a challenge to Romeo's house. Romeo's love for Juliet prevents him from quarrelling with Tybalt because he does not want to fight with his beloved's cousin, who has become his cousin by marriage. But his love for his friend Mercutio is powerful enough to turn into a rage of hateful revenge, so Romeo attacks Tybalt for killing Mercutio. For Juliet, the death of her cousin is a test of her love for Romeo. Which is stronger: her love for her family or for Romeo? As it turns out, her love for Romeo is strong enough to allow her to forgive him for his terrible deed, to choose her family by marriage, her husband, over her blood family. Juliet's love is further tested when she has to overcome her doubts about the trustworthiness of Friar Laurence and her fear of taking the potion. Again, her love is strong enough to risk everything. Romeo's love is strong enough to risk the Prince's punishment to get to Juliet's tomb. Both have love strong enough to be willing to die for the other, and they do. Thus, the whole play is a clash of passionate love and passionate hate, each strong enough to cause tragedy.

The Individual versus Society

A standard type of plot conflict, the individual against society, applies in *Romeo and Juliet* because the young couple is pitted against social and public institutions that are barriers to their relationship. First, of course, is the barrier of family, not only because Romeo and Juliet are from feuding houses, but also because Juliet's father has decreed that she will marry someone else. In Juliet's society, the father, as head of the household, has absolute power. Disobeying him means not only a breach within her family, but a breach of the social fabric that guides family structure in the culture. In fear of dire consequences, Romeo and Juliet have to marry in secret. They have to keep that secret from family and friends. Except for Friar Laurence, they have no one to rely on but each other. Even Juliet's devoted nurse turns on her and leaves her to make the biggest decisions of her life on her own. Finally, after Romeo is banished by the prince, even the local government is involved in keeping the pair apart.

The Problem of Time

While lousy timing fits into the theme of the action being determined by twists of fate, it is not just rotten luck that affects time in *Romeo and Juliet.* The chronology of the play is a rush of time. Romeo and Juliet are married the day after they meet. Romeo kills Juliet's cousin the same day and is banished from Verona only a day after the prince has first announced his intent to severely punish anyone caught fighting because of the Capulet/Montague feud. The couple has only one night of honeymoon before Romeo must run away, as Friar Laurence says,

> till we can find a time
> to blaze your marriage, reconcile your friends,
> Beg pardon of the Prince, and call thee back.

When Friar Laurence devises his plan to rescue Juliet, he needs time to get a message to Romeo, but that time is taken away when Lord Capulet moves up the date for Juliet's wedding to Paris. That change might not have been ruinous if Friar John had not been delayed on his way to find Romeo. There is so little time that the Capulet household stays up all night to prepare for the wedding that turns out to be Juliet's funeral. If only Friar Laurence had made it to the tomb in time, he might have been able to prevent Romeo from killing Paris and/or himself, which would have prevented Juliet from killing herself. But time is against them.

Topics for Further Study

- Romeo and Juliet is a story that ends with the suicides of the two teenage lovers. Research the extent of the problem with teenage suicide in the early 2000s and provide a list of resources for those seeking help.
- Juliet's parents try to arrange a marriage for her. What cultures in the 2000s still follow the practice of

arranged marriages?

- An important element in the story of Romeo and Juliet is the sword fights. In the early 2000s, sword fighting is known as the sport of fencing and is an Olympic event. Find out more about this sport and report on its modern practice and events.

- Could the tragic ending of *Romeo and Juliet* have been prevented? Cite some instances where a different action or turn of events might have saved the young couple. What would you have done in their place?

- Compare the tragedies of ancient Greek theater to those of Shakespeare. What are the differences and similarities? Specifically, what was new about *Romeo and Juliet* for a tragedy in its time period?

- Compare *West Side Story* to *Romeo and Juliet*. Match up the characters and the story lines. Comment on how Shakespeare's story has translated into a modern setting and conflict.

Fate and Forebodings

Elizabethans expected a tragedy to rest upon a twist of fate. Although Shakespeare made *Romeo and Juliet* more complicated than that, there are certainly numerous references to fate in the play, perhaps as a concession to the audience's expectations. The play opens with a reference to "star-crossed lovers" as if their fates are predetermined by their astrological signs. On the way to the Capulet party, Romeo has a sense that something will happen at the ball that will lead to doom. Later, with his dying breath, Mercutio calls a curse upon the feuding families: "A plague on both your houses!" Then Romeo says, after killing Tybalt, that he is "fortune's fool." When Romeo thinks that Juliet is dead, he tells the stars that he will defy them, as if he knows that fate wants to keep them apart, so he will win by joining Juliet in death. All the accidents of timing in the play seem to be fate working against the young lovers for the Elizabethan audience did not see these incidents as coincidences but rather as the hand of fate directing the action.

Style

Light and Dark Polarity Motif

A motif is a recurring element such as an incident, formulaic structure, or device that can help to develop and inform the text's major themes. A visual motif used in *Romeo and Juliet* is the contrast of light and dark, but in a sensory way, rather than in the sense of good and evil. For example, Romeo's balcony speech depicts Juliet as the sun that banishes the envious moon and turns night into day. In like manner, the morning after their wedding, they both try to delay Romeo's departure by pretending that it is still night, knowing that "More light and light, more dark and dark our woes." Ultimately, because the light of their love is not allowed to burn brightly, they both choose the darkness of death.

Shakespearean Tragedy

A Greek tragedy has one central heroic, but flawed, figure. *Romeo and Juliet* had two central characters, and neither is presented as having the characteristics of a classical hero. Prior to Shakespeare, Elizabethans used a twist of fate as the single causative factor for the tragic ending. Shakespeare, however, devised more complicated causes stemming from character traits and motives. Another difference between the Greek and

Shakespearean tragedies is the use of irony. In a Greek play, the audience is aware of the irony that the hero does not see. The chorus exists to advise the audience about what to expect. For example, the audience knows the secret of the parentage of Oedipus, but Oedipus does not and proceeds to marry his mother. Although Shakespeare uses a chorus in *Romeo and Juliet,* only the basic plot and ending were revealed, not how the drama is to unfold. Shakespeare allows the audience to discover the irony for themselves.

Use of a Chorus

Acts 1 and 2 only are introduced by the chorus, a lone actor who serves as a narrator for the play. The speech of the chorus is written in the form of a sonnet with an ending couplet. Shakespeare's prologue to *Romeo and Juliet* follows the Greek pattern of letting the audience know from the start how things are going to end. Otherwise, Shakespeare deviates from the Greek model by not revealing any of the irony or complexity of the tragedy, instead leaving that to the audience's own interpretation. The prologue of the second act assures the audience that Romeo's old feelings for Rosaline are gone and that he and Juliet now love each other. The chorus points out that although the couple has little opportunity to interact, their passion gives them the power and the ingenuity to get together. In other words, where there's a will there's a way if powered by love.

Blank Verse

The normal form of speech in Shakespearean drama is blank, or unrhymed, verse. This form of verse works well for all scenes and persons whose appeal is mainly to the emotions of the spectator or reader. Each unrhymed line has five stresses; however, Shakespeare subtly varied the stresses, as well as rhythms, pauses, and tones in order to convey different moods and even the personal peculiarities of a character.

Rhymed Verse

In the early plays, such as *Romeo and Juliet*, Shakespeare used quite a bit of rhymed verse in five-stress lines, usually in couplets. The prologues to Acts 1 and 2 end in a couplet, as does the play itself. Couplets also often come at the end of a scene or episode to signal changes to those behind the stage. In the process, the couplet achieves an aesthetic end to the dialogue and signals a change in action to the audience even before the actors leave the stage (e.g., act 1, scene 2, Romeo says, "I'll go along, no such sight to be shown, But to rejoice in splendour of mine own"). After a passage of blank verse or prose, rhymed verse could also have the effect of stiffening the dialogue and heightening the emotion. When Romeo and Juliet first meet, their dialogue becomes a sonnet, thus emphasizing the rise of their emotions. Shakespeare cleverly used rhymed verse for another effect—that of contrast—by having one character talk in blank verse while another uses rhymed verse.

Prose

The use of prose in a play that is mainly in verse has the effect of lowering the emotional level and quickening the pace of the play. Prose speech works best for passages of comedy and as the speech of the lower or more comic characters (e.g., the opening dialogue between Sampson and Gregory).

Historical Context

The Renaissance

Both the story of *Romeo and Juliet* and Shakespeare's life take place during the Renaissance, a period that begins in the fourteenth century and extends into the seventeenth century. The term renaissance means rebirth and refers to the revival of an interest in the classical cultures of Greece and Rome. However, there are many social, political, and intellectual transformations that comprised the Renaissance. As the influence of the Roman Catholic Church and the Holy Roman Empire waned with their inability to maintain stability and unity among the Europeans, the feudal structure broke up and the power shifted to nations that were developing their own monarchies and language. Also of great importance were city-states (e.g., Florence, Italy, as controlled by the infamous Medici family and perhaps fictional Verona as ruled by Prince Escalus). Many details in *Romeo and Juliet* connect it to Italian Literature with which Shakespeare was familiar. One parallel is Pyramus and Thisbe (Ovid). More immediate, Shakespeare probably based his play on the Italian version by Luigi da Porto who sets the tale of Romeo and Juliet in Verona (1530).

During the sixteenth century, ancient Greek and Roman literature was rediscovered, translated, and then widely read. The classical writers focused on the human condition; they explored human nature and asserted some valuable insights about what causes human suffering and what works to establish social order. These ideas, along with many others, converged as a philosophy called humanism. It was in the broadest sense a focus on human beings as opposed to a focus on the supernatural. Renaissance writers such as Shakespeare were well-read in classical literature and were influenced by it. In one sense, *Romeo and Juliet* dramatizes how an inherited feud coupled with impetuosity can disrupt the state and ruin good people's lives. The play shows that passion can be disruptive, dangerous, and destructive, and yet ironically it also expresses love and grief. Through the loss of these two young lovers, the feuding familes find reconciliation, and order in the community is reestablished. This examination of the human scene is an example of humanism with clear connections to classical handling of tragedy, as in *Oedipus* by Sophocles and *Pyramus and Thisbe* by Ovid.

Elizabethan and Jacobean Literature

By the time Shakespeare was born, Elizabeth I was already on the throne. Her long and influential reign from 1558 to 1603 defined the era. As a playwright, Shakespeare was fortunate to write in a time when the arts were supported by patrons and his English contemporaries included Ben Jonson,

Sir Walter Raleigh, Christopher Marlowe, Robert Southwell, Thomas Campion, Edmund Spenser, Sir Philip Sidney, John Lyly, and Michael Drayton, all important writers, critics, and celebrities of the Elizabethan Age whose reputations have lasted into modern times. There are numerous and diverse distinguishing characteristics of Elizabethan literature. This name is strictly a time division in honor of one of England's greatest rulers. However, it is a time in which the poetry of the sonnet, the Spenserian stanza, and dramatic blank verse were very popular. It is unquestionably a golden age for drama. In the area of prose, this era produced historical chronicles, pamphlets, and literary criticism as the first novels began to appear. The tone of literature seemed more darkly questioning during the reign of James I as writers explored the problem of evil. This was the time in which Shakespeare produced his greatest tragedies. His theatre company enjoyed a cordial relationship with the court where the popularity of the masque, an extravagant courtly entertainment, returned. Also during Jacobean times (Jacobean is the name of the period in which James I reigned in England), Jonson influenced comedy with an acid satire and poetry with a lucid and graceful style that was copied by a group of writers known as the Cavalier poets. Meantime, Francis Bacon and Robert Burton were making a name in prose literature with a tougher yet more flexible style. Jacobean literature was undoubtedly an important contribution to the arts, but perhaps the greatest achievement of the age was the production of the King James version of the

Bible in 1611.

Compare & Contrast

- **1300s:** Chaucer receives great acclaim in his own lifetime (1343–1400) from both the British public and the royal court for writing the *Canterbury Tales* and other poetic works.

  1590s: Shakespeare starts his career in the London theaters and enjoys popular success from the beginning, even garnering the favor of Queen Elizabeth I.

  Today: Both Chaucer and Shakespeare are still considered to be geniuses of literature by people around the world, and their works are studied as part of the standard curriculum in most schools.

- **1300s:** The papacy leaves Rome and is located in Avignon, France from 1309 to 1377 because of political pressures from the French. The first rumblings of the Reformation are heard in England from John Wycliffe.

  1590s: The Reformation is in full swing. The conflicts between Protestants and Catholics are often violent, and European countries align according to Protestant or Catholic affiliation.

Today: The world still struggles with religious conflicts. Protestants and Catholics have reached accord in many areas, except for some tension yet in Northern Ireland. However, Muslim extremists wage a holy war in many areas of the world, and some governments forbid religion entirely.

- **1300s:** In 1346, the Black Death kills almost a third of the people of Europe and Asia.

    1590s: Plague closes the theaters in 1593, and other such diseases pose a deadly threat. Elizabeth I barely survives small pox, and Shakespeare later succumbs to a mysterious fever.

    Today: The plague and small pox are virtually eliminated around the world. Other new contagious diseases such as the ebola virus and AIDS have arisen, but where modern medicine is available, the potential for an epidemic is minimized.

- **1300s:** Important innovations are the blast furnace, the standardization of shoe sizes in England, and, at the end of the century, the Dutch use of windmills.

1590s: The first knitting machine is invented as well as the first flush toilet. Coal mining begins in Germany, and scientists begin to investigate magnetism and electricity.

Today: Technology and computers are universal, and technology witnesses advances occurring so quickly that some equipment is outdated within months of installation.

Critical Overview

Even after four hundred years, literary criticism of Shakespeare's *Romeo and Juliet* and critical reviews of its productions are still being written. Nonetheless, the critical essays written through the centuries remained valid and illustrate how interpretation is affected by various literary movements. Oddly enough, Shakespeare's contemporaries did not review the plays, and other writers barely mentioned him well into the seventeenth century. At that time, Ben Jonson (1572–1637) was held in higher regard as a playwright. Also esteemed as a critic, Jonson considered Shakespeare a talented, but undisciplined writer, according to Augustus E. Ralli in his book on Shakespearean criticism. John Dryden, a seventeenth-century writer, was the first great Shakespearan critic. In his "An Essay of Dramatic Poesy," Dryden compares Shakespeare and Jonson, saying that he admires Jonson but loves Shakespeare because "when he describes anything, you more than see it, you feel it too." Even though he praised Shakespeare, Dryden also found he was "many times flat, insipid, his comic wit degenerating into clenches, his serious swelling into bombast."

Critics into the eighteenth century continued this view that Shakespeare had more natural ability than educated refinement. They discussed his artistic faults rather than his merits, unless they were pulling out those soliloquies and other passages that they thought could stand on their own out of context. In 1775, Elizabeth Griffin commented on the ample selection of "poetical beauties" in *Romeo and Juliet*. However, she found little for moral evaluation except the foolishness of a young couple embarking on plans of their own without the consent of their parents. Thus, Griffin was the first critic to lay the blame for the tragedy not on fate but on Romeo and Juliet.

Even more than Shakespeare, the eighteenth-century neoclassicists believed strictly in the unities of place, action, and time, which Aristotle explained in his *Poetics*. Thus, these critics thought the story of a play should take place in one setting; have a causally connected plot, each event causing the next one in line; and that all of these events should occur within one twenty-four hour day. Samuel Johnson, a moderate neoclassicist and the prime literary figure of his time, excused Shakespeare from these three unities. He found *Romeo and Juliet* to be one of Shakespeare's most pleasing dramas and found the plot varied, believable, and touching. He also thought Shakespeare correct to mix tragedy and comedy because real life is a mixture. Still, Johnson was one of those critics who felt that Shakespeare's work lacked sufficient moral emphasis. Ralli reports that Alexander Pope, another leading eighteenth-century writer and critic, theorized that Shakespeare's genius was dragged down by his involvement with actual theater production, implying that Shakespeare wrote to please the audiences instead of according to the structures of classical rhetoric.

Meanwhile, in Germany, August von Schlegel and others were finding *Romeo and Juliet* to be nearly perfect artistically. Schlegel said of this play: "It was reserved for Shakespeare to unite purity of heart and the glow of imagination, sweetness and dignity of manners and passionate violence, in one ideal picture." Back in England, Samuel Taylor Coleridge, considered a great nineteenth-century Shakespearean critic, began to share the German view. Coleridge suspected that Shakespeare's irregularities were actually evidence of psychological and philosophical genius. William Hazlitt, another Shakespearean critic of the English Romantic movement, was also an admirer of Schlegel. Hazlitt attributed more depth to the love of Romeo and Juliet than previous critics who found their love shallow and sentimental. Following Hazlitt's lead, by the end of the eighteenth century, Shakespearean scholarship began examining the playwright's techniques of characterization.

In the nineteenth century, criticism associated Shakespeare's genius with many intellectual movements and religious theories. Suddenly, Shakespeare no longer had faults but presented intriguing problems for the astute scholar to explain. In the twentieth century, New Critical scholars searched for something new to say, focusing on minute textual details in order to come up with new theories or interpretations. It is to the credit of the Romantics, however, that they returned to a discussion of the sheer enjoyment of the plays that audiences experienced. In the early 2000s, Shakespeare's works continued to be read, performed, and critiqued by scholars around the world. After all this time, criticism had become a blend of schools of thought and argued interpretations based on new information found by researchers or new approaches connected to advancing theoretical understanding. Generally speaking, though, it is safe to say that Shakespeare is considered the greatest playwright of all time.

Sources

Abrams, M. H., ed., *The Norton Anthology of English Literature,* 5th ed., Vol. 1, Norton, 1986, pp. 1845–47.

Brooke, Stopford A., *On Ten Plays of Shakespeare,* Constable, 1925, pp. 35–70.

Coleridge, Samuel Taylor, *Shakespearean Criticism,* 2d ed., Vol. 1, edited by Thomas Middleton Raysor, Dutton, 1960, pp. 4–11.

Dryden, John, "An Essay of Dramatic Poesy," in *The Norton Anthology of English Literature,* 5th ed., Vol. 1, edited by M. H. Abrams, W. W. Norton, 1986, pp. 1845–47.

Griffin, Elizabeth, *The Morality of Shakespeare's Drama Illustrated,* reprint, Frank Cass, 1971, pp. 495–99.

Griffith, Kelley, Jr., *Writing Essays about Literature,* Harcourt Brace Jovanovich, 1986, p. 72.

Hazlitt, William, *Characters of Shakespeare's Plays and Lectures on the English Poets,* Macmillan, 1903, pp. 83–94.

Johnson, Samuel, *Johnson on Shakespeare,* edited by Arthur Sherbo, Yale Edition of the Works of Samuel Johnson, Vol. 8, Yale University Press, 1968, pp. 939–57.

Jorgens, Jack J., *Shakespeare on Film,* Indiana University Press, 1977, p. 85.

Ralli, Augustus E., *A History of Shakespearian Criticism,* Vol. 1, Oxford University Press, 1932, pp. 21–22.

Snider, Denton J., *The Shakespearian Drama, a Commentary: The Tragedies,* Sigma Publishing, 1887, p. 78.

Ulrici, Hermann, *Shakespeare's Dramatic Art: History and Character of Shakspeare's Plays,* translated by L. Dora Schmitz, Vol. 1, George Bell and Sons, 1876, pp. 381–97.

von Schlegel, August Wilhelm, *A Course of Lectures on Dramatic Art and Literature (1809–11),* translated by John Black, Henry G. Bohn Publishers, 1846, pp. 400–01.

Witherspoon, Alexander M., and Frank J. Warnke, eds., *Seventeenth-Century Prose and Poetry,* 2d ed., Harcourt Brace Jovanovich, 1963, pp. 118–19.

Further Reading

Asimov, Isaac, *Asimov's Guide to Shakespeare: A Guide to Understanding and Enjoying the Works of Shakespeare,* reissue ed., Gramercy, 2003.

> Well-known scientist Asimov clarifies the complexities of Shakespeare with explanations, synopses, and information about the mythological, historical, and geographical backgrounds of Shakespeare's works.

Bloom, Harold, *Bloom's Notes: William Shakespeare's "Romeo and Juliet,"* Chelsea House Publishers, 1996.

> Harold Bloom, an authority on Shakespeare, provides very brief but excellent "notes" with biographical and bibliographical information, character and structural analysis, and excerpts from some of the best criticism through the years on *Romeo and Juliet.*

Dobson, Michael, and Stanley Wells, eds., *The Oxford Companion to Shakespeare,* Oxford University Press, 2001.

> This book covers biographical information, literary criticism, historical and cultural information,

> and much more about Shakespeare and his works. The plays are given scene-by-scene explanations as well as other notes.

Gervinus, G. G., *Shakespeare Commentaries,* translated by F. E. Bunnett, rev. ed., 1877, reprint, AMS Press, 1971, pp. 204–29.

> Gervinus, a well-known German Shakespearean critic of his time, looks at the poetry of *Romeo and Juliet* as well as what he considers the central theme of passion. Gervinus thinks Friar Laurence is Shakespeare's mouthpiece in the play.

Goddard, Harold Clarke, *The Meaning of Shakespeare,* University of Chicago Press, 1960.

> Goddard writes essays about Shakespeare's plays that are insightful and opinionated and full of ideas to provoke thoughtful consideration of Shakespeare's genius.

Guizot, M., *Shakespeare and His Times,* Harper and Brothers, 1852, pp. 161–73.

> Guizot criticizes the contrast between the innocent and ideal feelings that Shakespeare shows in *Romeo and Juliet* and the unnatural, ill-fitting language that Guizot thinks

are used to express them.

Kermode, Frank, *The Age of Shakespeare,* Modern Library, 2004.

> This book is a good overview of the life of Shakespeare, the influences of the age in which he lived, and the practices of the theater at the time.